Original title:
Branches and Banter

Copyright © 2025 Creative Arts Management OÜ
All rights reserved.

Author: Maxwell Donovan
ISBN HARDBACK: 978-1-80567-326-2
ISBN PAPERBACK: 978-1-80567-625-6

## The Side-splitter of the Sidra

In a grove full of glee,
A cat climbed a tree,
Slipped on a limb,
And fell with a whim.

Birds laughed from above,
With a chirp and a shove,
While squirrels joined in,
To bask in the din.

A wise old owl quipped,
As he nearly flipped,
"If you can't take the fall,
Stay off the tall!"

The sun set in jest,
As laughter was blessed,
In a dance of delight,
As day turned to night.

## Emerald Enthusiasms

In a field painted green,
A frog jumped unseen,
He tripped on a leaf,
And caused quite the grief.

Grasshoppers leapt high,
With a chuckle and sigh,
They joined in the fun,
'You should've just run!'

Flowers started to sway,
In their colorful play,
A bee buzzed along,
Singing a silly song.

Under cloud-puff delight,
They danced through the night,
In a world full of cheer,
With giggles so near.

## Laughter Encapsulated in Green

Behind the thick bush,
A raccoon made a push,
To snag a nice snack,
And gave quite a whack.

The berries all squished,
As laughter was wished,
The critters did cheer,
In a humorous sphere.

A turtle then slowed,
On his perilous road,
He joked with a sigh,
"Why be fast? Just lie!"

In this vibrant domain,
No worry, no pain,
Just folly and fun,
Under the warm sun.

## The Camaraderie of Canopies

Under a wide tree,
Where shadows agree,
A squirrel stole nuts,
And ran with swift cuts.

The branches did sway,
As friends joined the play,
With a giggle and wink,
They rarely would think.

The breeze joined in too,
With a humorous cue,
As leaves softly danced,
In laughter, they pranced.

In this leafy retreat,
They shared jokes so sweet,
A friendship so bright,
That sparkled with light.

## Echoes of the Orchard

In the orchard where fruits hang low,
Apples giggle at the wind's soft flow.
Pears whisper secrets, ripe and round,
While plums toss jokes from the ground.

The cherries crack up, rolling in row,
As the breeze joins in with a playful blow.
An orange throws a punchline so sweet,
While laughter ripples at the trees' feet.

Squirrels tumble, crafting their schemes,
Their antics dance on sunlit beams.
Each branch shakes with a chuckle and cheer,
Echoes of joy that all creatures hear.

So come sip the nectar of humor's delight,
In the orchard where laughter takes flight.
With every bite, a giggle you'll taste,
In this happy haven, none goes to waste.

## Jest and Jangle in the Grove

In the grove where shadows play,
Lemons and limes jive all day.
Breezes blow through leafy glee,
With every rustle, a comic spree.

A raspberry swings from a twig so thin,
Cracking jokes while dangling in.
The nuts all laugh, they roll so fast,
Bouncing around, joy unsurpassed.

Bright bluebirds chirp in silly tune,
Dancing on the branches, under the moon.
Their feathers shimmer, a riot of sound,
In this bustling, vibrant playground.

With laughter echoing 'neath every bough,
The grove's a stage for the merry crowd.
Join the revels, don't give it a miss,
In this jangle of jest, pure bliss.

## Under the Green Canopy

Underneath the leafy shade,
Witty vines have plans laid.
A cucumber winks and nods in delight,
While carrots gossip about leafy fright.

The peas burst forth with playful chime,
Spinning tales of olden time.
With moles and bugs joining in jest,
Each moment shines, oh so blessed.

A rabbit hops with a bounce and twist,
Swapping quips that can't be missed.
As sunbeams tickle the forest floor,
Nature's laughter, forevermore.

So settle down, let your worries flee,
Under this canopy, wild and free.
Embrace the mirth that life can yield,
In this vibrant, joyous field.

## Leafy Laughter

Among the leaves where stories weave,
Frogs croak jokes nobody believes.
Sunflowers spin, grinning wide,
In the joyful chaos, none can hide.

The twirling breeze stirs up some fun,
As ladybugs join the picnic run.
With ants in hats and grasshoppers prance,
A spontaneous jig breaks out in a dance.

A wise old tree shakes its bark,
Sharing anecdotes in the dark.
And every whisper, every shout,
Keeps the laughter circling about.

So come and join, let your heart be light,
In this realm where glee takes flight.
Join the chorus of giggles and cheer,
In the world where merriment is near.

## Mirth Beneath the Foliage

In a leafy patch where squirrels thrive,
A rabbit hopped in, oh how he strived.
He tripped on a twig, let out a squeak,
The laughter that followed was quite unique.

An owl perched high, wise in his gaze,
He chuckled at antics through leafy maze.
Unseen moss danced, in silent delight,
As critters below sparked humor in light.

Breezes carried whispers, giggles in flight,
A worm in a hat joined in the light.
With each little jibe, the sun shone anew,
Creating a party among every hue.

Under the canopy, with spirits so high,
Life's little blunders made everyone sigh.
So gather your friends, let the antics unfold,
In this patch of joy, the laughter's pure gold!

## Jests in the Treetops

High above the ground, a parrot played,
With a ruffled up tune, a tune he betrayed.
He mimicked a cat, whose meow turned to roar,
It left all the monkeys giggling galore!

Squirrels were plotting a feast full of nuts,
But were met with acorns thrown from their huts.
A raccoon chimed in, with a grin on his face,
Declaring the nut wars, a wild, wacky race.

On a branch swing, a sloth took a nap,
But his dream brought a bat with a cap on his flap.
They both made a mess, as they swayed to and fro,
And sent all the critters into fits with their show!

There's laughter that rings in the trunks overhead,
As stories of jest, take flight where they spread.
So laugh with the leaves, let your worries all go,
In treetops of humor, the heart starts to glow!

## Tales of the Timber

In the heart of the woods where the giggles reside,
A fox made a joke while the badger just eyed.
He slipped on a leaf and tumbled with flair,
The humor contagious, it floated through air.

At a table of logs, a feast had begun,
With mushrooms for chairs, oh what silly fun!
A porcupine served, with toothpick in paw,
Declared, 'Here's a dish from my quilled, fancy law!'

Grasshoppers chirped, joining in the jest,
Their bouncing revealed the very best fest.
With each little quirk, the laughter grew bright,
Under timbered skies, a charming delight.

So come one and all, join this merry spree,
For tales of the timber take root in glee.
Every chuckle and snort makes the forest alive,
Where friendship and humor together thrive!

## Fragments of Fun in the Thicket

In a thicket so dense, a hedgehog proclaimed,\n'Life's too short, so let's get untamed!'
He juggled some berries, slipped on a vine,
And laughter erupted, oh how divine!

Amidst tangled roots, the chattering grew,
A rabbit shared tales no one else knew.
With wild stories spun, and grins that were fleet,
The thicket transformed into quite the grand feat!

A pixie flew by, with mischief in mind,
Sprinkled some glitter, with giggles aligned.
A frog leaped in shock, then joined the wild scene,
In fragments of fun, they all felt like queens.

So dance with the shadows, let laughter enfold,
For joy in the thicket is richer than gold.
With each quirky story, hearts flutter and twine,
Creating sweet moments, where joy is divine!

## Promises Beneath the Bark

In a grove where secrets hide,
Lies a tree with arms stretched wide.
It whispers jokes to passing bees,
About the funny things in trees.

Squirrels giggle, jumping high,
While rabbits pause with curious eye.
They share their tales from dawn till dusk,
With leaves that dance and twigs that rust.

The owl hoots with a knowing grin,
Tales of mischief held within.
Beneath the bark, laughter grows,
In every nook, a story flows.

So gather round, oh friends so dear,
Let's listen close, for laughs are near.
For in this wood, where dreams embark,
Lies a treasure—promises of lark.

## **Murmurs Between the Foliage**

Leaves rustle softly in the breeze,
Talking nonsense with such ease.
The sunbeams smile through branches wide,
Crafting shadow games to bide.

The chipmunks gossip, cheeky and spry,
Sharing secrets with the sky.
A daring crow, with a caw so loud,
Claims the title of the funniest shroud.

The petals giggle, pink and bright,
As they twirl in sheer delight.
With each breeze, they tease and sway,
Promising laughter in their play.

So venture forth, dear friends of mine,
Where mischief grows like tangled vine.
In every rustle, every cheer,
Murmurs of joy are always near.

## Tales from the Arbor

Once a tree told tales quite grand,
Of silly sprouts from fertile land.
With roots that wiggled like a jester,
It teased the flowers, the merry investor.

A woodpecker chimed in with beak,
Delivering puns of every week.
With flaps and flutters, it turned so spry,
Making branches laugh and sigh.

Fungi joined with a quirky dance,
Provoking laughter—take the chance!
They tripped on roots and rolled with glee,
Creating capers beneath the lea.

So gather 'round, let stories flow,
In this verdant lair where giggles grow.
With tales spun high and spirits free,
The Arbor's joy's for you and me.

## Dialogue in the Dappled Light

In the glen, a chatter's started,
With beams of sunlight, laughter imparted.
Grasshoppers leap, discussing schemes,
While sunflowers nod in gleeful dreams.

A hedgehog claims a diamond hat,
While listening ears perk for a chat.
Ants march in, a comical parade,
Trading quips in the cool, green shade.

The shadows whisper secrets sly,
As butterflies flutter and flutter by.
In dappled light, the fun ignites,
With every glance, a burst of sights.

So weave your words in joyous flight,
Among the trees, where there's delight.
In every giggle, every spark,
There's magic shared beneath the bark.

## Laughter in the Grove

In the shade where whispers play,
Squirrels dance the day away.
Beneath the leaves, a giggle grows,
As breezes tickle, laughter flows.

A crow drops jokes in jesting flair,
While rabbits form a courtly pair.
Their chatter mixes with the breeze,
As sunlight dapples through the trees.

The fox adds puns with every step,
While frogs recite their finest prep.
With silly hops and merry quirks,
They share their tales, their laughter works.

In this grove, where humor blooms,
Each creature shares its quirky tunes.
With every chuckle, joy extends,
As nature laughs, and all pretends.

## Echoes of the Forest

Echoes bounce from tree to tree,
As wise old owls sip their tea.
With every hoot, a punchline flies,
Tickling truth beneath the skies.

The deer in caps, they tell tall tales,
Of epic runs and windy gales.
Their laughter rings through leafy halls,
While chipmunks cheer and the chatter sprawls.

Playful shadows dance on ground,
As playful banter swirls around.
The breeze joins in with a gentle sigh,
As sunbeams giggle, dancing high.

In twilight's glow, the echoes play,
Filling hearts with bright array.
With every chuckle, the night descends,
In the forest, all humor blends.

## Twigs and Tittle-tattle

Twigs a-twirl in breezy spree,
As gossip flows from tree to tree.
The hedgehogs swap their wildest lore,
While crickets hum and dance for more.

With whispered tales of nighttime fun,
They giggle softly, one by one.
A raccoon snacks on dreams delight,
Sharing secrets under starlight.

Beneath the boughs, the stories spin,
Of silly blunders and wild whims.
Their laughter echoes through the night,
As woodland creatures share their light.

So gather close, let's share a jest,
In nature's arms, we find our best.
With twigs and tattle, we unite,
As joy ignites and dreams take flight.

## Conversations Under the Sky

Underneath the vast expanse,
The birds conspire, break their trance.
With flirty chirps and cheeky winks,
They share their secrets, laugh, and think.

The butterflies wear silly hats,
While bumblebees outsmart the cats.
With every buzz, they tease away,
Creating joy, come what may.

The frogs sit round, a toady crew,
Swapping tales of what they knew.
With every leap, a laugh erupts,
In silly scripts their joy constructs.

As stars blink down, the magic grows,
With every story, laughter flows.
In nature's chat, we find delight,
Beneath the sky, the world feels right.

## Whispers in the Canopy

In the treetops, jokes take flight,
Squirrels chuckle, what a sight!
The wind tickles leaves with glee,
Nature's stand-up, wild and free.

Birds conspire with sneaky twirls,
Sharing secrets with the swirls.
A wise old owl hoots with flair,
Telling tales beyond compare.

A raccoon joins with playful flair,
Joking 'bout the food laid bare.
The branches sway with every pun,
Laughter echoes, oh what fun!

Above the ground, where giggles soar,
Each rustling leaf shouts for more.
In this haven, joy takes root,
As nature shares its playful loot.

## **Laughter Among the Leaves**

The leaves whisper in sunny beams,
Tickling ears with wild dreams.
Frogs croak jokes on lilypad stools,
While bees buzz in silly pools.

A nut falls down, a soft thud sound,
Making all onlookers astound.
A chipmunk snickers, 'Gotcha there!'
With a wiggle and a jump to spare.

Upper branches swing, lightly sway,
Where giggles chase the dawn's first ray.
Every bud a laugh enriched,
In this green stage, we're all bewitched.

Underneath, the roots join in,
Giggling softly, like a grin.
This leafy crowd, in joy they trust,
In each chuckle, we find the rust.

## Conversations Under the Boughs

Underneath the tangled vines,
A chorus of chuckles intertwines.
Leaves flutter like hands in cheer,
As the woodland chatters loud and clear.

The bushes burst with giddy snorts,
With cheeky creatures playing sports.
A foxtrot dance, a squirrel's wink,
What do they say? Oh, let's not think!

The shadows play a game of tease,
Echoing laughter on the breeze.
A turtle cracks a timeless joke,
While all around, the laughter strobes.

With each whisper from the ground,
Humor thrives where joy is found.
In this refuge of mirthful spells,
Nature's jesters, who cast their wells.

## Chatter in the Arbor

In an arbor where chatter swirls,
A parade of giggles, twirls.
A parrot squawks a silly rhyme,
Timing perfectly, every time.

The branches twist, the woodland grins,
Sharing secrets where laughter begins.
In the shade, shadows tease the light,
Mocking the day, such a delightful sight!

A hedgehog's snicker, such a sight,
As fireflies flicker with pure delight.
"Did you hear that?" a voices sings,
"Such weight in humor, look at these wings!"

And all around, the fun expands,
As echoing giggles clasp their hands.
In this merry nook, so joyous and bright,
Every chatter feels just right.

## Fables of Flora

In a garden where daisies play,
A sunflower told a tale one day.
"Why did the tomato blush so red?"
"Because it saw the salad dress!"

A dandelion puffed with glee,
"I can blow a seed far as can be!"
But a cheeky breeze came swirling past,
And scattered dreams a bit too fast.

An ant strolled by with a grand hat,
Said, "I'm off to fight a giant rat!"
But tripped over roots that were quite sly,
And landed right where the ladybugs lie.

So let's giggle at garden life,
Where leaves and laughter banish strife.
Each bloom has stories, some absurd,
In the whispers of nature, they're all heard.

## Tales from the Twisted Trunks

Beneath the old oak's wrinkled guise,
A squirrel shared secrets, full of lies.
"I once saw a tree that could dance!"
It spun on its roots, gave nuts a chance.

A wise old willow with hair so long,
Said, "Listen to wind; it sings a song."
A passing raccoon could barely hear,
"What's that rustling? Is dinner near?"

The birch laughed loud at its own white bark,
"Ever tried to be a pop star, hark?"
With a wig of leaves, it sang a tune,
That made even the crows gather soon.

In the forest, where whimsy thrives,
Every twist and turn brings funny vibes.
Nature's tales, in silence spun,
Are treasures of laughter, never done.

## The Folly of the Foliage

In the thicket, where the green things grow,
A fern said, "I'm putting on a show!"
It jived with the moss and giggled a lot,
While the lilacs laughed from their sunny spot.

A hedgehog claimed it could climb up high,
"Just watch me reach for the blue sky!"
But tangled in thorns, it fell with a thud,
"I prefer my ground…that's just how I'd bud."

The ivy wove tales of mischief grand,
"I took a stroll and tripped, oh man!"
With tendrils that swooped and snared a hare,
Who blinked in surprise, half caught in air.

So in this jungle of green and cheer,
Nature tells tales you must lend an ear.
For every sprout and every vine,
Is a story of fun, in its own twine.

## The Chorus of the Trees

In the meadow, trees do sway,
Squirrels chatter, on display.
A parrot jokes, it's quite absurd,
Laughter echoes, how we've heard!

Breezes tickle leaves in play,
Whispers giggle, come what may.
Roots below, the secret keep,
Under moonlight, giggles leap!

Branches twist in playful dance,
Critters frolic, take a chance.
A raccoon wears a silly hat,
While owls hoot, "What's up with that?"

In the forest, glee ignites,
Life's a jest, with merry sights.
Join the fun, let laughter steer,
In nature's realm, we hold dear!

## **Rejoice Among the Roots**

Underneath the oaken crown,
Worms are wriggling, wearing frowns.
Mice share tales of cheese gone wrong,
Chortling loudly, joining the throng.

Beneath the soil, the fungi giggle,
While ants march, they dance and wiggle.
A crow drops jokes, slick and sly,
"Why can't the tree run?" Oh my, oh my!

Grasses sway, with glee they wave,
Telling secrets, bold and brave.
While flowers blush, unable to hide,
At pollen puns, they take great pride!

Oh, the roots shake with so much glee,
In the earth, the fun's a spree.
Nature's humor, rich and vast,
In this realm, our smiles last!

## Ramblings of the Rustic

On a fence post, an old cat sits,
Wags her tail, and throws some fits.
"Why can't the crow find his way home?"
"Because he lacks a map to roam!"

Cows complain of grass too high,
While chickens gossip, oh my, oh my!
Pigs quip jokes about the mud,
Together they laugh, rolling in the crud.

A breeze blows by, tickles the field,
With every twist, the laughter's revealed.
Thus, within the rustic lands,
Friendships flourish, just as planned.

Barrels roll with gentle sound,
Rustic life, where joy is found.
Nature's jesters, all around,
In this laughter, love is bound!

## Jive in the Jungle

In the jungle, colors bright,
Monkeys dance with sheer delight.
Tigers tell their funniest tales,
While parrots soar on windy trails.

Vines swing low, giving chase,
Creepy crawlies join the race.
A bear winks, his jokes in tow,
"Why did the lizard cross, you know?"

A chorus of critters, loud and proud,
Bantering beneath a leafy shroud.
Every creature wears a grin,
In this party, where fun begins.

Dancing under the moonlit glow,
Rhythms pulsing, fast and slow.
Together we weave tales so grand,
In this jungle, hand in hand!

## **Ramble Through the Glade**

In the glade where squirrels play,
Chasing shadows, come what may.
They chatter loud, a silly song,
While dancing leaves take turns along.

A chatty bird with vibrant plume,
Sips nectar sweet, a floral bloom.
It twirls and twists in playful jest,
While frogs sing low, their croaked request.

The breeze joins in, a gentle tease,
Whispering secrets through the trees.
With every rustle and laugh shared,
Nature's antics, thoroughly bared.

So wander here with lightened heart,
Where laughter thrives, a joyful art.
In this glade, let spirits lift,
For in mirth lies the brightest gift.

## Joyful Soundscape of Nature

Listen close to the nature's hum,
A chorus of chirps, a joyous drum.
Bunnies bounce on soft green grass,
While time's sweet laughs, a quickened pass.

The crickets plan their evening show,
With tap-tap-tapping, they steal the flow.
As fireflies twinkle, a radiant dance,
Inviting all, come take a chance.

The brook giggles as it flows,
Telling tales that no one knows.
While clouds above shape funny hats,
And tease the trees with gentle chats.

So join the pace, the merry sound,
Where giggles rise from the soft ground.
In nature's realm, find playful bliss,
A joyful web that none can miss.

## Banter of the Branches

Up in the trees where the silly vines,
Trade playful barbs and funny lines.
They sway in laughter with every breeze,
Beguile the sun with a wink and tease.

A squirrel quips, 'I'm faster still!
Catch me if you can, oh, what a thrill!'
While leaves giggle in vibrant hues,
Responding quick like the morning dew.

Nearby a crow caws with wise old glee,
'What's in a twig? Come see, come see!'
The branches nod, they share a gaze,
And sway in rhythm, lost in praise.

Banter unfolds with every rustle,
A playful bond, no need to hustle.
In this realm where green meets sky,
Every laugh echoes, bold and spry.

## Whimsy in the Weald

In the weald, where the wild things thrive,
The stories and giggles come alive.
Mischievous elves trip over roots,
While giggling buds adorn their suits.

The brook sings songs of ancient lore,
While deer prance lightly, seeking more.
With every jump, a ticklish breeze,
Makes daisies shake, join in with ease.

The shadows dance beneath the sun,
Winking at all, a playful run.
A wise old owl cracks jokes at night,
As wisps of fog spin silvery light.

So wander through this enchanted space,
Where laughter and beauty intermingle with grace.
In the weald, let your spirit soar,
For whimsy and joy are never a bore.

## Joy in the Branching Paths

Upon the twisting limbs we swing,
A squirrel's tale, he starts to sing.
With acorn hats, they plot and plan,
As nature's jesters, oh, what a clan!

The robin twirls on a lofty chair,
A feathered jester without a care.
He tells the leaves to join the spree,
And dance like they're all feeling free!

A breeze whispers secrets, cheeky and bold,
As kites in the sky do break the mold.
While wise old owls roll their eyes,
At the silliness under sunny skies.

The laughter rings through the forest green,
Where critters share jokes, quite the scene.
In this cheerful realm, just take a look,
Nature's own storybook has it all hooked.

## Fluttering Fables of the Trees

A butterfly's waltz flits to and fro,
While the frogs croak stories we long to know.
Each leaf has a tale, each twig has a pun,
In this leafy kingdom, oh what fun!

The woodpecker knocks with a tap-tap-tap,
While the fox rolls by in a goofy nap.
"Hey, Mr. Owl, what's wise today?"
He hoots back, "Just waiting for some prey!"

With vines that twist and twirls that spin,
The laughter of critters brings joy from within.
As clouds parade with a fluffy grin,
The world comes alive, let the games begin!

The sun plays hide and seek with glee,
While shadows dance like it's a jubilee.
From trees to the ground, a grand tableau,
Nature's laughter is the best show.

## **Amusement Amidst the Leaves**

In a cozy nook where the branches sway,
A chipmunk glances, "Is that all you say?"
The sunbeams chuckle as they filter through,
Whispering jokes that are fresh as dew.

The dancing shadows bring smiles all around,
Where every rustle is a joyous sound.
Like little pixies on a wild spree,
The laughter here, it runs so free!

A snail in a race, oh, what a sight!
Takes hours to finish but feels just right.
The ladybugs gather, all dressed in red,
Sharing secrets with the daisies' head.

With every breeze comes a playful tease,
Nature invites us to join in with ease.
So if you wander through this leafy embrace,
Expect to wear joy, it's a merry place!

## **Nature's Lighthearted Duet**

Two owls hoot in their duet so sweet,
While the clumsy raccoon trips on his feet.
"Why did you stumble?" one wise voice calls,
"Trying to dance and forget my falls!"

The wind joins in with a playful gust,
Tickling the trees, shushing their rust.
A chase ensues with a sprightly hare,
And the creatures giggle, floating in air!

With acorns as maracas, they shake and sway,
A concert of critters, come join the play!
Every chirp and chuckle fills the warm breeze,
In this symphony of laughter, nature's tease.

When day bids farewell, colors start to gleam,
The moon smiles wide, joining in on the dream.
Amidst the branches, where laughter thrives,
With every naughty jest, joy comes alive!

## **Silliness in the Sunbeams**

Under rays where laughter grows,
Ticklish toes and funny nose.
Juggling shadows, they collide,
As silly whispers start to slide.

A dog in shades, all bark and cheer,
Sipping tea while others leer.
Chasing clouds that giggle back,
In this place, there's no lack.

Butterflies in bow ties dance,
While the daisies take a chance.
To trick the bees with jokes galore,
As laughter spills from every pore.

So raise a toast to sunshine bright,
Where every day is pure delight.
And if you trip, just take a bow,
For joy is lost if we don't allow.

## The Vine's Verses

Twisting tales on laden vines,
Each grape bursts with funny lines.
Tangled roots and giggling leaves,
Sprouting puns that no one grieves.

A squirrel draped in leafy flair,
Pulls faces, thinking no one's there.
While laughter rolls on earthy trails,
Chasing wind that tells tall tales.

The dew drips laughs from every bud,
As flowers chuckle in the mud.
In this garden where we roam,
They're planting seeds of jest for home.

So sip the nectar, raise a cup,
For joy is sweet, never give up.
And let the whimsy spill and swell,
In this vine, all stories dwell.

## **Puns in the Pines**


In the woods, where whispers tease,
Pines are full of pranks, not fees.
A raccoon wears a tiny hat,
While squirrels chatter, "What of that?"

Tree trunks twist with silly glee,
Giving every passerby a free.
Jokes hidden in the knots they keep,
While forest secrets never sleep.

Every rustle, every snap,
Shares a punchline, oh what a chap!
Beneath the boughs, we all unite,
In laughter's glow, we're feeling right.

So let's climb high and holler loud,
Among the branches, giggling proud.
For in this wood, all smartly pine,
The humor grows, like aged fine wine.

## Mirth Beneath the Mulberry

Underneath the berry tree,
Laughter ripens, wild and free.
With juicy puns and playful jive,
Each laugh helps the berries thrive.

The birds join in with tweets and chirps,
As ants parade with silly jerks.
A picnic spread where pies abound,
Fueling giggles all around.

Each grappling vine knows the score,
As mischief dances at the core.
Sticky fingers reach for more,
Playing tricks they can't ignore.

So let us feast on mirth today,
For in this grove, we laugh and play.
With every bite and chuckle shared,
Joy multiplies, and none are spared.

## Jests of the Wildwood

In the woods, the squirrels scheme,
Acorns tossed in a merry dream.
The rabbits laugh, their ears all perked,
As wind blows softly, a joke correctly worked.

The owls hoot with a wise old grin,
While raccoons plot where the fun begins.
A dance of shadows, a nightly show,
Nature's jesters, stealing the glow.

Frogs croak tunes, a ribbit of cheer,
While crickets chirp for all to hear.
The foxes tiptoe on laughter's trail,
In every rustle, a funny tale.

So join the frolic, the woodland cheer,
With giggles and chuckles ringing clear.
The trees may whisper, but can't contain,
The light-hearted fun in the wild refrain.

## Puns of the Pines

Underneath the pines so tall,
The needles giggle, a gentle sprawl.
A porcupine with a quill-tipped pun,
Tickles the branches, oh what fun!

The pinecones scatter, a playful tease,
As a wind-swept whisper dances with ease.
A chattering chipmunk, quick on its feet,
Cracks a joke, oh isn't it sweet?

A lizard lounges, sunbathing with flair,
Countless puns floating, light as air.
With every rustle the laughter flows,
As pine trees nod, the humor grows.

So gather 'round for the jokes untold,
In this forest of laughter, so bright and bold.
The punchlines echo, a natural rhyme,
With nature as comedy—oh, what a time!

## Gossip in the Garden

In the garden, secrets bloom,
Petals giggle, dispelling gloom.
The daisies whisper behind their backs,
While tulips gossip in flower-packed racks.

A bumblebee buzzes, a curious spy,
Eavesdropping on the roses nearby.
The pansies blush and sway so neat,
As vines entangle, sharing the sweet.

Veggies chuckle, roots intertwined,
A lettuce leaf, with jokes well-defined.
They trade tales of sun and rain,
In this plot where laughter reigns.

So join the chatter, the merry spree,
With nature's laughter as your decree.
In the garden alive, let joy take flight,
With whispers and giggles, pure delight!

## Larks in the Limbs

Perched on high where the breezes sway,
The larks share jokes in a merry display.
With wings a-flutter and chirps so bright,
   They laugh at clouds drifting light.

A squirrel scurries, signed in jest,
As the sun dips low, the day's at rest.
Bouncing branches echo in cheer,
With each little quip, the world feels near.

The sky is canvas where comedy weaves,
With colorful hues, like autumn leaves.
Their silly squawks paint stories anew,
   Of simple joys in every view.

So listen closely, let laughter ring,
Amongst the limbs, the songs of spring.
With feathered friends raising a toast,
To every giggle, we cherish most.

## The Revelry of the Reeds

In the meadow, reeds sway low,
Dancing giggles in the flow.
Beneath the sun, a cheeky play,
Whispers of mischief lead the way.

Frogs croak jokes, a soft delight,
While crickets chirp both day and night.
A breeze carries laughter near,
As nature's jesters spread good cheer.

Tails of rabbits twitch with glee,
Chasing shadows, wild and free.
Each rustle hides a giggling friend,
In the grassy shindig, never end.

With every sigh, the reeds enjoy,
Nature's antics, like a toy.
Sunset brings the curtain down,
Yet echoes of laughter wear the crown.

## Snicker Under the Shrubs

Underneath the leafy shade,
Sneaky whispers, jokes well-laid.
Squirrels chatter, jesters bold,
In this green world, laughter's gold.

Bumblebees buzz a silly tune,
Each flower giggles, in full bloom.
With every rustle, a prank to behold,
Stories of mischief, forever told.

A snail slips past, wearing a grin,
As butterflies spin, their twirls begin.
The shrubs play host, a comedy stage,
Nature's laughter, timeless as age.

When shadows stretch, oh what a scene,
The whispers dance, so unforeseen.
Beneath the bushes, joy ignites,
In this green haven, pure delight.

## Mirth of the Cypress

Tall the cypress, swaying proud,
Cackling softly, a lively crowd.
Gales of wind, a tickle here,
Nature's humor drawing near.

The owls hoot at the comical night,
Chasing shadows, what a sight!
Each rustle speaks of jokes anew,
A symphony of laughter, bright and true.

With each creak of the wood, they tease,
Breeze tips over, like a sneeze.
A parade of laughter fills the air,
In the arms of the cypress, joy to share.

When dawn breaks, giggles persist,
Sunlight spills on morning mist.
The cypress sways, still full of cheer,
A tall guardian of laughter dear.

## Scribbles of the Sycamore

The sycamore paints doodles high,
With leafy hands and a playful sigh.
Scribbles dance against the sky,
Jolly lines that twist and fly.

Each sunbeam bends to catch a joke,
As shadows play, and branches poke.
In the rustling leaves, a tale is spun,
A tapestry of giggles, full of fun.

Beneath the trunk, a game unfolds,
Where squirrels share secrets untold.
They leap and spin, a merry crew,
In nature's theater, laughter's due.

At twilight's close, the breezes sigh,
With whispers of joy that never die.
The sycamore stands in jest and lore,
In every leaf, a chuckle's core.

## Sylvan Stories

In the realm of trees, tales take flight,
Squirrels debate the best nut in sight.
Owls roll their eyes at the crow's loud boast,
While the breeze chuckles, a playful ghost.

Fungi gossip in their patchy attire,
While rabbits plot mischief by mossy pyre.
A woodpecker drums a beat so absurd,
Even the shyest rabbit's now heard.

The dappled sunlight plays hide and seek,
As crickets crack jokes that flutter and squeak.
Nature's own stage, where laughter takes root,
In every whisper and each playful hoot.

So listen closely to the forest's cheer,
For every rustle holds a tale sincere.
In the company of trees, fun finds a way,
To fill the woodland with joy every day.

## The Laughter of Leafy Friends

Leaves chuckle softly at the wind's sly tease,
While ants in a row sing hymns with much ease.
Bees buzz around with tales of delight,
Making flowers giggle, what a splendid sight!

The hedgehogs snicker at the snail's slow pace,
As rabbits hop in a merry race.
A butterfly jokes as it flits to and fro,
Saying, "Why walk when you can put on a show?"

Mice whisper secrets near the old oak trunk,
While foxes glare in the spotlight, quite punk.
With their furry tales swaying in the breeze,
The woods are alive with hilarity's tease.

In this leafy haven, laughter does sprout,
A melody of joy that swirls all about.
So let every rustle and giggle combine,
For here in the grove, it's always party time!

## **Rituals in the Understory**

Under the canopy, a dance starts to bloom,
Tiny toadstools gather, dispelling the gloom.
With a wink and a wiggle, they twirl with great flair,
While mushrooms dip low, really quite debonair.

The hedgehogs form pairs, a conga line tight,
As chipmunks on drums keep the beat just right.
Squirrels swing by, with nuts in their paws,
Competing for laughter, they break all the laws!

With a flick of a tail, the raccoons take charge,
Pulling pranks from their pockets, they dance and enlarge.

The laughter is bubbling as bugs join the throng,
Each buzzing note adds to their joyful song.

And as night falls, with stars sparkling bright,
The creatures still banter, a whimsical sight.
In this underworld of giggles and cheer,
Their soul-stirring laughter fills hearts, oh so dear.

## Banter of the Buds

In the garden of whispers, a seedling does poke,
Its clever retorts cause the petals to choke.
"Why stand so still, when you can sway with grace?"
And daisies reply, "We prefer a slow pace!"

The tulips giggle at the rose's grand hues,
While violets chime in, sharing tongue-in-cheek news.
"Your perfume's too sweet for a night on the town!"
They tease and they laugh, never wearing a frown.

Frogs croak a melody, calling all near,
While bees buzz with glee, making mischief appear.
With every quip and chuckle so spry,
The humor flows light like clouds in the sky.

So let the buds chirp, keep the joy ever bright,
For laughter is golden, in day or in night.
In this whirlwind of fun, all know they belong,
In a patch of pure joy, where the heart sings along.

## The Dance of the Boughs

In the sway of the trees, they twist and shout,
Leaves giggle in whispers, with joy they sprout.
A squirrel spins tales, with acorns to share,
While the wind chimes in with a ruffled hair.

Around and around in a playful fling,
Laughter's the song that the branches all sing.
The sun winks down, casting shadows that sway,
As nature plays tricks in a light-hearted way.

With every soft rustle, there's mischief afoot,
Buds tease the blossoms with comical soot.
A bad pun from a robin, who lands with a hop,
Makes all of the blossoms chuckle and pop.

So join in the fun, let your worries release,
Each twist of the boughs brings a moment of peace.
In this comedic wood, where laughter's the goal,
Nature's the jester, and joy fills the soul.

## Jest in the Thicket

In the thicket so thick, where the shadows loom,
A rabbit tells jokes to brighten the gloom.
The hedgehog chortles, with a snicker or two,
While the trees arch their backs to get a good view.

A fox prances in, with a swagger and grin,
"Have you heard about squirrels? They're all nuts in their kin!"
The laughter erupts, like a bubbling brook,
As the critters all gather, with mischief and hook.

The owl hoots a pun, in that wise, wily way,
"Why don't trees play poker? They're afraid of a stray."
And under the leaves, a chorus of glee,
Echoes the joy of this raucous spree.

In the heart of the thicket, the jesters convene,
Crafting giggles and gaffes, so vibrant and keen.
Each rustle a punchline, each breeze brings a cheer,
In this whimsical realm, we forget all our fear.

## Secrets of the Saplings

Tiny sprouts giggle, with secrets to share,
Beneath sun-drenched skies, they toss out their flair.
Chasing the sunbeams, they wobble and sway,
Each new little leaf has a joke on display.

"Why did the twig refuse to play charades?
It couldn't find anyone who knew all the grades!"
Laughter erupts, like a breeze through the grove,
As saplings unite in this jestful alcove.

The old oaks just chuckle, with wisdom so grand,
"Just give them a moment; they'll all understand!"
And giggling in unison, they dance on their roots,
Like little green jesters in whimsical suits.

The secrets of saplings, like whispers of mirth,
Bring joy to the soil and laughter to earth.
With each playful sway, and each rustle they make,
The world feels much lighter, for laughter's awake.

## The Hum of the Wilderness

In the hum of the woods, a chirp takes the lead,
With a beat in the branches, they gather with speed.
A lizard struts proudly, in scales of bright green,
Cracks jokes to the vines, who all giggle and preen.

"Did you hear what I heard?" a grey jay calls out,
"Said the flower to spring, 'You bring all the clout!'"
The resonance dances, on breezes so light,
As the laughter unfurls, it takes flight in delight.

With a rustle and flutter, the creatures partake,
Every chuckle a ripple in clear rippling lake.
The sunbeams join in, casting gold on the fun,
As the wilderness hums under light of the sun.

So come to the wild where giggles abound,
Each step is a laugh, and mirth re-sounds.
In the symphony of life, feel the joy in your chest,
As nature spins tales that will always bless.

## Whimsy in the Woodland

A squirrel wore a tiny hat,
It danced with joy, what a funny cat!
The owls took bets on who'd win
In the race from trunk to generous grin.

The acorns giggled on the ground,
As teetering twigs spun round and round.
A worm proclaimed, 'I am the king!'
While ants all cheered, 'Now that's a thing!'

A rabbit joked of twinkling snails,
Who told tall tales of wind-filled sails.
The trees cackled in leafy glee,
As night brought forth their symphony.

In the hush, a shadow crept,
The raccoon laughed, "I'm well-kept!"
With playful pranks and merry cries,
Nature's jesters wore moonlit ties.

## The Arbor's Lighthearted Confessions

A cheeky crow confessed today,
He'd stolen snacks—what a faux pas play!
The woodpecker laughed, with a tap-tap show,
'It's better to share than to holla "no!"'

The deer strutted, antlers high,
'Look at me, I can nearly fly!'
The bushes shook with muffled mirth,
A chuckling echo filled the earth.

The rabbits giggled on the lane,
As frogs croaked out a silly refrain.
While fireflies twinkled in delight,
Creating art across the night.

A breeze would tease, a shiver prance,
Nature's jesters in a daring dance.
With laughter ringing through each bar,
The woods held joy, both near and far.

## Whispers Among Leaves

The leaves were sharing secrets sweet,
A chipmunk danced on furry feet.
'Did you hear what the sparrow said?'
'Oh do tell, I'm hanging by a thread!'

A playful breeze made branches sway,
While butterflies began their play.
'What's the news from the shady grove?'
'A turtle won! He never troved.'

The hedgehogs snickered in soft grass,
'Did you watch the snail that moved fast?'
They spun their tales of clumsy flight,
And laughed aloud till the fall of night.

Then stars peeked through with twinkling eyes,
As nature shared her gentle sighs.
In whispers soft, their giggles blend,
A world alive where humor won't end.

## **Chatter in the Canopy**

The parrots squawked tales quite absurd,
Of a goose who mimicked every word.
'You think you're clever?' the magpies chortled,
As peeking raccoons giggled, unscorched.

With mismatched socks on a branch so high,
A sloth declared he could touch the sky.
With lazy grins and a wink to show,
His dreams unfolded, lovely and slow.

The squirrels debated who was the best,
Rolling acorns as they took a rest.
With laughter bright and silly games,
They shared their shocking, wacky claims.

As moonlight draped the forest sway,
Each critter chuckled in full display.
In this green realm where jests fly free,
Who knew a tree could be so witty?

## Folklore of the Flora

In a garden wild, a tale was spun,
Where daisies dance and laughter's begun.
The sun wore shades, a sight to see,
While bumblebees buzzed in harmony.

A cucumber spoke, with wits quite sly,
'The carrots can't play, they're just too shy!'
The daffodils chuckled, petals aflutter,
And whispered sweet jokes, oh, how they stutter!

'Would you tell that rose to stop making fuss?
It's just jealous, not one of us!'
The tulips chimed in, their colors so bold,
Spinning yarns of the garden, wonders untold.

As the dusk painted skies with hues so rare,
The flora would gossip, without a care.
In laughter and joy, they'd spin the night,
In this enchanting grove, oh, what delight!

## **Verdant Voices**

The oak had a story that warmed the air,
Of a squirrel who thought he was quite debonair.
With acorns as hats, he'd strut and prance,
While leaves whispered softly of his clumsy dance.

The ferns exchanged gossip, tucked in the shade,
About flowers in bloom who'd slightly delayed.
'Why so late, dear bloom? Did you lose the plot?'
The sunflower grinned, 'I forgot my dot!'

Even the mushrooms joined in the game,
With a riddle or two, no one felt shame.
'The secret to growing,' the fungi would tease,
'Is never to worry, just sway with the breeze!'

As twilight draped green in a silken wrap,
The laughter erupted, like a bright gentle clap.
Nature's own chorus, in giggles and plays,
Echoed through meadows, in whimsical ways.

## The Gathering of the Grove

In the heart of the woods, where the giggles reside,
The critters convened, oh what a lively tide!
The rabbits brought snacks, fresh carrots, of course,
While the owl hooted softly, a wise, steady force.

The hedgehog spun tales of adventures he'd braved,
Of slipping on moss, how he chuckled and waved.
The fish in the brook chimed in with a splash,
'Our stories are best, come listen, we clash!'

A gathering of trees, with whispers so light,
Critiqued every creature through day and through night.
The acorns dropped wisely, a laughter-filled rain,
Mixed with chirps and brief howls, a harmonious chain.

So now, every dusk, in the grove they convene,
With joy and with jest, in a world evergreen.
Their echoes of laughter float high and wide,
In a place where all critters share hearts open wide.

## Romp Through the Reflection

In reflecting pools where the dragonflies dart,
The lilies chuckled, 'What a strange art!'
A frog in a tux sang a tune on the shore,
While the weeping willow swayed, wanting more.

'You think you can leap? You're just too full of glee!'
Cried the fish with a wink, 'Dive in, you will see!'
The pond laughed back, its ripples a dance,
As the frog took a plunge, decided on chance.

'The ripples are secrets, they tickle and tease,
What fun to be splashed by a soft summer breeze!'
The sunbeams laughed low as the clouds joined in,
Casting shadows of silliness, grins stretched like skin.

As twilight approached, the stars winked with glee,
The reflections would linger, as wild as the sea.
In echoes of water, where all spirits play,
Laughter would ripple, come night or come day!

## Sprightly Fronds

In the garden, whispers play,
A leaf tickles a bloom all day.
The sunbeams dance with joy and cheer,
While shadows giggle, ever near.

A squirrel chatters, up on high,
While curious buds peek at the sky.
With every breeze, secrets unfold,
A tale of mischief, bright and bold.

Pollen sneezes, "Achoo!" it shouts,
While daisies laugh, oh, what a clout!
The grasshopper plays a tune so spry,
Who knew the flowers could dance and fly?

With every rustle, laughter roars,
As petals swing on invisible shores.
While bumblebees buzz side to side,
A lighthearted world, their joyful ride.

## Nature's Dialogue

A robin flutters, calls a friend,
While daisies lean, the gossip to lend.
"Did you hear?" the tulips inquire,
"About the worm with dreams to aspire?"

The sun spills giggles like watered vines,
Butterflies laugh, sipping sweet wines.
"Oh look," says one, "a snail in a race!"
"What's the hurry?" the daisies embrace.

The creek chuckles, bubbling with glee,
"Why hurry when you can float like me?"
A rabbit snickers, twirls in delight,
As shadows stretch and embrace the night.

Every leaf swirling in playful jest,
Calls forth the moon for a skyward fest.
Through whispers and laughs, the forest sings,
A merry meeting of earthly things.

## **Leafy Laughter**

In leafy halls, the chatter grows,
Where acorns plot and mischief flows.
"Let's roll downhill!" a brave sprout cries,
While elder oaks just roll their eyes.

A lizard snickers, sunning all day,
While ferns sway, encouraging play.
"Why so serious?" the blossoms plead,
"Join the fun, and follow our lead!"

Raindrops giggle, patter, and ping,
As frogs join in, ready to sing.
The sunlight breaks with a goofy grin,
Bouncing off leaves, oh, what a spin!

With every flutter, laughter flares,
In nature's realm, joy freely dares.
Through joyful rustles, all unite,
In a cheerful, leafy delight.

## The Chuckle of the Cattails

By the water, cattails sway,
Sharing stories of the day.
"Did you see how that frog jumped high?"
"Right over that lily!" a bulrush sighs.

The dragonflies zip, playing tag,
While reeds sway, never to lag.
"C'mon!" calls one, "let's race the breeze!"
And they giggle, as quick as you please.

The pond reflects a silly face,
As the fish splash, a joyful lace.
"Who's the king of this watery throne?"
"Let's spin a tale—who needs a phone?"

With each ripple, the laughter flows,
Echoing softly where the wild grows.
Nature's fun, a great parade,
In every sigh, a joke is made.

## **Noteworthy Notes from Nature**

In the woods, a pine asks a birch,
'Why do you sway? Are you at church?'
The birch just laughs, 'No, just for fun,'
'Twirling in circles under the sun.'

A maple joins in with a silly jig,
Says, 'I'm the star! Watch me now, dig!'
The lilac pipes up with a flowery shout,
'How do you think I keep the bees about?'

The oaks just chuckle, wise and stout,
'It's all in the roots; that's what it's about!'
The pines roll their eyes, 'Why are we here?'
The answer's simple: laughter, my dear!'

With whispers and giggles from all around,
Nature's jokes echo, oh what a sound!
Together they sway, with spirits so bright,
In the forest of fun, they dance through the night.

## The Merry Maples

In fields of gold, the maples shout,
'Tell a tall tale! It's what we're about!'
One claims to have grown the biggest leaf,
The others burst out, 'What a belief!'

Another one boasts of its sweetest sap,
While squirrels below hang on like a chap.
'Oh no, my friends, the trick is the sun!
Without proper shade, we won't have our fun!'

One maple grins, 'Shall we form a band?
We'll sing to the wind and dance on the land!'
The others agree, with laughter they twirl,
Creating a ruckus that makes the world swirl.

So in the bright woods, a concert takes flight,
With maple melodies that echo through night.
Nature's fine jesters, they never stand still,
Raising a ruckus, oh what a thrill!

## Conversations in the Clearing

In the clearing bright, under skies so wide,
Two hedges gossip, with whispers they bide.
'Have you seen a leaf wearing a hat?'
'Only on Tuesday, now imagine that!'

A thicket joins in, 'What about shoes?
I heard the stumps have joined active crews!'
Then out from the bushes, a crow takes flight,
'You trees are daft, don't you see the light?'

But the elders just laugh, roots deep as can be,
'Life's all about fun, you must agree!'
A wildflower chimes, 'With colors so bright,
Who needs a story when we're here for the night?'

So they share their coy jokes, and bursts of delight,
In the vast, open clearing, laughter takes flight.
Together they scheme and weave silly tales,
Nature's own comedy that never pales.

## Chit-chat by the Meadow

Down by the meadow, the daisies delight,
Chatting in circles till the fall of night.
'That butterfly's awful; it thinks it's the best!'
'Hey now, don't be rude, it's merely a guest!'

The clovers all chuckle at the bluebottle's dance,
'It spins quite a lot, does it think it's a prance?'
But one wise old daisy pipes up with a grin,
'Let those who can dance, oh let them begin!'

A patch of wild grasses sways in reply,
'The more that you twirl, the closer to the sky!'
Insects join in with a buzz and a hum,
The meadow's alive, oh what a fun drum!

With laughter and love in the soft evening air,
The daisies, the clovers, the grass, all laid bare,
In their colorful chatter, a joy pure and sweet,
Together they thrive, their lives a warm beat.

## **Playful Shadows of the Trees**

Under the sun, shadows dance,
Whispering secrets in a glance.
Leaves are giggling, find the tune,
As squirrels plot their nutty boon.

Tickling breezes push and pull,
While branches sway, the air is full.
A chat between the boughs and sky,
I hear a crow making a sly reply.

The grass below joins in the fun,
Rolling around as bright leaves run.
Each wobble and wiggle speaks so clear,
Nature's jesters, come gather near.

In this tangled web of mirth,
Life unfolds, revealing worth.
Laughter echoes, loud and bright,
In the woods, all feels just right.

**Dialogue of the Wild**

Listen close, there's chatter near,
Critters gossip, never fear.
The brook's a judge with a gurgle grand,
While ants march on, a troop so planned.

A bunny bites into a snack,
While chirping birds give wisdom back.
"Did you see the fox?" one feathered sage,
"Swift as lightning, he's quite the rage!"

In the thicket, a raccoon shares,
His latest scheme and wild affairs.
The owls hoot their sage advice,
"Wise up kids, don't roll the dice!"

Each rustle brings a fresh debate,
Under the trees, they cogitate.
A symphony of chatter spins,
In nature's tale, everyone wins!

## Between the Twigs

Peeking through the leafy veil,
A cheeky squirrel tells a tale.
"Did you hear what happened last night?"
A rustle sounds, oh what a fright!

The busy bees buzz and tease,
Trading gossip with the breeze.
The wise old owl shakes his head,
"I'd rather nap instead," he said.

Mix and mingle in the shade,
Every creature's got it made.
The ladybug flips through the chat,
"Just don't mention the hungry cat!"

In this canopy of jest and cheer,
Nature's laughter rings so clear.
Join the fun, come take a peek,
Between the twigs, it's never bleak.

## The Language of Limbs

Watch the limbs weave a sweet word,
As breezes carry tales absurd.
A wave from elm, a bow from pine,
In this chatter, all is fine.

The oak, so bold, tells tales of yore,
While willows murmur, limbs implore.
"Join us here," they seem to sing,
In nature's court, there's much to bring.

With rustling leaves that giggle lightly,
And branches swaying ever sprightly.
It's a gathering, don't you see?
In the woods, we're wild and free.

So come on down, bring your smile,
Stay for a while, let's reconcile.
In the language of the trees so grand,
Laughter blooms across the land.

## **Revelries in the Woodlands**

In the grove where the squirrels play,
Acorns drop with a funny sway.
Frogs croak jokes that never land,
While raccoons dance, holding hands.

Breezes tickle the feathered crew,
With whispers of secrets known by few.
Trees giggle with leaves in the breeze,
As owls hoot puns with perfect ease.

Bunnies hop, sharing silly tales,
While hedgehogs spin in their tiny gales.
Mice play cards in the soft moonlight,
With fireflies glowing, oh what a sight!

Every nook and cranny's alive,
With laughter that makes the forest thrive.
So join the fun, don't be shy,
In the woodlands where spirits fly!

## The Chatter Beneath the Bark

Underneath the great old tree,
Listen close, it's full of glee.
Woodpeckers tap their raucous tune,
While gossip flows from dawn to noon.

Squirrels exchange the latest scoop,
As turtles join the chattering troupe.
Each whisper tickles the bark's ear,
With tales of pranks that cause good cheer.

Mice discuss the best cheese found,
While hedgehogs roll with laughter's sound.
The breeze carries jokes toward the sky,
Witty repartees that won't run dry.

Fungi giggle, sprouting with flair,
Mushrooms know all, they're quite the pair.
In this chatty grove, with joy we bask,
Nature's secrets, no need to ask!

## Harmony in the Hollowed Trunks

In hollowed trunks, the crickets sing,
A symphony of joy, what fun they bring!
Ladybugs share their fashion tips,
While ants perform their dance, no slips.

Fireflies flash as stars come to play,
Lighting up paths in a whimsical way.
Old tortoises tell their sagas long,
While the wind hums nature's favorite song.

Laughter echoes through leafy lanes,
Where raccoons prance like they've got no chains.
Nature's tune is a jovial blend,
With friends all around, where smiles extend.

So let's gather 'round and join the sound,
As merriment blooms in the green surround.
Each hollow trunk holds a tale to tell,
In the laughter of woods, we all dwell!

## **Frolic in the Field of Greens**

In fields where the daisies skip and sway,
Bunnies play hopscotch all day.
Butterflies giggle, swirling in flight,
While grasshoppers crack jokes, a delightful sight.

The sunbeams sparkle, bringing delight,
As toddlers of nature play in pure light.
Roots tickle the toes of the wandering deer,
With laughter echoing, crisp and clear.

Caterpillars race, quite slow but spry,
While ticks remind them to never be shy.
Ladybugs jest, sharing berry grams,
As frogs join in with splashes and jams.

In this haven of greens, fun never ends,
With every corner, a new joke descends.
Nature's playground, where hearts brim and beam,
Join in the frolic, live the dream!

## The Bantering Bud

In a garden of giggles so bright,
A flower wears a hat just right,
The bees all buzz with tales to share,
While blooms wink back without a care.

A dandelion plans a prank on the breeze,
It tickles the nose with such perfect ease,
The petals laugh, they dance and sway,
As the sun grins wide at their display.

Worms are wiggling, plotting a tease,
To tell the roots their paths with ease,
"Watch out for puddles, they're not too deep!"
"Unless you're a toad, you'll take a leap!"

In every corner, laughter flows,
As nature's humor endlessly grows,
With colors bright and spirits high,
The joy of life, we can't deny.

## Lively Leaves

In the wind, the leaves are dancing,
With whispers low and secrets prancing,
They nudge the branches, a friendly shove,
"Let's drop a shadow, it's what we love!"

A squirrel scampers in a wild chase,
The leaves erupt in giggling grace,
"Catch him quick before he slips,
On acorns rolling, let's see those flips!"

The sun plays peek-a-boo with the shade,
While critters gather, a jovial parade,
"Oh look, it's a flower, all dressed in dew,
Let's tease it till it brightens too!"

Together they spin in the breezy air,
A whimsical mix, a lively affair,
Each rustling sound tells a joke untold,
In nature's playground, joy can't grow old.

## **Ribaldry of the Rainforest**

In a thicket where nonsense reigns supreme,
A parrot yells, "Hey, wake from your dream!"
The toucans cackle, with colors bold,
"Join our ruckus, don't be so cold!"

A sloth hangs low, with a lazy grin,
"Life's but a joke, let the fun begin!"
The monkeys swing with a cheeky shout,
"Grin and bear it, there's no doubt!"

Frogs in chorus croak such tunes,
Stirring up laughter beneath the moons,
"Oh look, a snail just dashed right past,
Is it a race? Who could have guessed?"

In this vibrant land where joy takes flight,
Every creature shares in the light,
With each laugh, the world feels anew,
In ribaldry, they thrive and pursue.

## Nature's Chuckle

A pebble rolled down a hill with glee,
"Where's the hurry? Just roll with me!"
The grass sways low, with a whispered jest,
"It's best to take life, just like a rest!"

A butterfly flutters, with wings all aglow,
"Look at me dance, I'm the star of the show!"
The daisies nod, as they wiggle and sway,
"Let's share our petals, brighten the day!"

"Why did the twig laugh at the tree?"
"Because it split its trunk—oh, can't you see?"
All nature chortles at silly old sights,
In mirthful moments, they scale new heights.

So here we find, among plants and sun,
That laughter's the thread that ties everyone,
For in this realm of humor and cheer,
Nature's chuckle is always near.

## Whispered Wits and Wonders

In the shade of gossiping trees,
Squirrels plot their mischief with ease.
A parrot squawks jokes, his feathers bright,
As laughter dances in the soft twilight.

A raccoon in a mask starts to tease,
About the owl's obsession with cheese.
The bunnies giggle, hiding in the grass,
While the wise old tortoise says, "Let's pass!"

The wind carries secrets as it flows,
Tickling the leaves, where mirth just grows.
Each rustling whisper, a playful shout,
In nature's realm of gleeful rout.

Beneath the boughs, where silliness reigns,
Every twig bends with whimsical chains.
So here we gather, let laughter fly,
In this playful glade, where joy is nigh.

## The Enchanted Exchange

In the heart of the forest, two foxes meet,
Swapping stories and tales, oh so sweet.
One wears a hat, the other a scarf,
As they chuckle and snicker, their laughter is far.

The rabbit hops in, with a dramatic flair,
Pretending to faint in the middle of air.
The hedgehog laughs, rolling on the ground,
While the trees sway, with giggles profound.

A wise old owl shares a riddle or two,
"Why did the chicken cross? Oh, who knew?"
The animals chuckle, some snort with delight,
In this realm of whimsy, all feels just right.

As stars peek through the emerald veil,
Echoes of laughter ride the night's trail.
They toast with acorns, a cheer to the night,
Embracing the humor that fills them with light.

## Exchange of the Elder

An ancient tree leans close to its friends,
Whispering wisdom as the day begins.
With roots deep in laughter, it sways to the tune,
Of the critters below, a merry commune.

The wise old badger shares tales of the past,
Of days when the forest was not such a blast.
The chipmunks roll over, they've heard this before,
Yet still, there's a chuckle, they always want more.

A pair of raccoons joins the chatter so bold,
Juggling shiny trinkets, their antics unfold.
The elder tree chuckles, its branches shake free,
As laughter cascades like leaves from the spree.

With every chuckle, a sprinkle of cheer,
Undercover giggles, a room full of dear.
In this jovial gathering, wisdom flows free,
Embracing the fun, in sweet harmony.

## Humor in the Hollow

Deep in the woods, where shadows play right,
Lives a gathering of friends, all full of delight.
A squirrel cracks nuts, then dances a jig,
While fireflies twinkle, lighting the gig.

A badger in glasses recites a fine tale,
Of how he once tried to outrun a snail.
The critters roar laughter, their sides start to ache,
As they picture the hurry of that slow little make.

One wise old frog croaks out a funny croon,
About the last party they held in June.
Frothy around edges, he makes them all grin,
As fun fills the hollow, let the laughter begin!

At night, stars embrace this jolly old crew,
United by giggles and tales born anew.
In the heart of the forest, humor does dwell,
In hollows of merriment, they frolic so well.

## **Lighthearted Exchange in the Forest**

Oh, the oak asked the pine, so tall and spry,
"Why do you sway like you're dancing nearby?"
The pine just chuckled and said with a grin,
"It's the breeze, my friend, it's got me in spin!"

The maple chimed in, with colors so bright,
"I've got stories of fall, oh what a sight!"
The birch rolled its eyes, a bark full of sass,
"Like we need more talk; your leaves are a mess!"

The willow whispered sweetly, "Let's just be clear,
It's the critters that gossip, far more than we hear!"
As the squirrels laughed on, making a fuss,
The forest roared back with a warm, merry gust!

In this lively grove, where the humor flows,
Each tree shares a laugh, as the wild wind blows.
In a world full of chatter, be it bark or a song,
It's the joy of the woods that keeps us all strong!

## Humor Woven in the Vines


In the garden of life, where the tomatoes glare,
The beans play tag, who would dare to care?
The squash said with a giggle, "I'm losing my pride,
With all this vine-tangling, I'm being denied!"

The peppers burst out, all shiny and bright,
"Let's have a taste test, who's packing the bite?"
The corn proudly stood, tall with a grin,
"With popcorn at stake, I'm sure to win!"

With laughter and jokes, they twirled in the sun,
A veggie brigade, all in good fun.
The cucumbers chuckled, a pickle in hand,
"In this veggie gossip, we're a funny band!"

As moonlight shone down, they danced and they sang,
In this patch of humor, the night sweetly rang.
When life feeds you laughter, don't let it stray,
In vines of humor, we'll play every day!

## The Gossiping Glade

In a glade where the breezes whisper and tease,
The flowers gossip softly, rustling like leaves.
"Did you see that bee? Oh, what a show!"
"He's never on time, it's how he does flow!"

The daisies all nodded, their heads in a sway,
"With petals like mine, he just can't delay!"
A daffodil quipped, with a laugh like a chime,
"If buzzing were fashion, he wouldn't be prime!"

"Let's plant a new tale," the rose did declare,
"Of butterflies swooning in elegant air!"
But violets just blushed, with a giggle and glance,
"We all know that fluttery heart's lost in chance!"

As the sun settled down, they shared in delight,
In this chatting glade, all made wrongs feel right.
Where blooms spread the joy, like a fragrance so sweet,
In laughter and gossip, life is a treat!

## Quips and Quirks in the Wilderness

In the woods where the whimsy plays leapfrog with light,

The critters compare their odd habits at night.
"Oh, the raccoon's been digging, it's nutty and wild,
While the owl just hoots back, looking quite riled!"

The fox with a flair, always thinks he's so sly,
"Did you see how he jumped? Just a blink and a fly!"
The rabbit chuckled, munching on greens,
"Kinda like that time you got stuck in those beans!"

With a snap of a twig, the laughter erupts,
While the deer raised their heads to see who interrupts.
"We're all just a quirk, in this wild, wacky game,
How else could we be? None of us is the same!"

Under stars full of shimmer, they share tales and jest,
In this patch of the wild, not a worry or quest.
In every wise crack, and each chirp and quire,
Lies a bond of good fun, that the woods so inspire!

www.ingramcontent.com/pod-product-compliance
Lightning Source LLC
Chambersburg PA
CBHW070751220426
43209CB00083B/754